It's either working for you or someone else

By

John R. Keuffer, III C.C.C.W.
Richard Carey
Kathy Garrison

Assisted by

Mark Wooten
Jim Beck
DJ Sutton

Order this book online at www.trafford.com
or email orders@trafford.com

Most Trafford titles are also available at major online book retailers.

"Money Matters™" is a trademark of Teen Response, Inc. and John Keuffer, Richard Carey, Mark
Wooten and Kathy Garrison, denoting a series of products that may include but is not limited to
books, pocket cards, calendars, audio cassettes, DVD's and other materials.

Note for Librarians: A cataloguing record for this book is available from Library
and Archives Canada at www.collectionscanada.ca/amicus/index-e.html

Printed in Victoria, BC, Canada.

ISBN'S: 978-1-4269-1346-4 (Soft)
ISBN'S: 978-1-4269-1347-1 (Dust)

Library of Congress Control Number: 2009931987

*We at Trafford believe that it is the responsibility of us all, as both individuals
and corporations, to make choices that are environmentally and socially sound.
You, in turn, are supporting this responsible conduct each time you purchase a
Trafford book, or make use of our publishing services. To find out how you are
helping, please visit www.trafford.com/responsiblepublishing.html*

*Our mission is to efficiently provide the world's finest, most comprehensive
book publishing service, enabling every author to experience success.
To find out how to publish your book, your way, and have it available
worldwide, visit us online at www.trafford.com*

Trafford rev. 8/14/2009

 www.trafford.com

North America & international
toll-free: 1 888 232 4444 (USA & Canada)
phone: 250 383 6864 ♦ fax: 812 355 4082 ♦ email: info@trafford.com

PRAISE FOR MONEY MATTERS

"I give my strong support for the MONEY MATTERS ™ program...As principal of Woonsocket Middle School, I can personally attest to the success and impact that this program has had on our students...this program has been extremely successful at WMS and I hope that other districts will have this opportunity..."

-Dr. Patrick McGee, Principal
Woonsocket Middle School

"It gave me ideas that I can use in my own life."

-Jenna-Lea Behrens
St. Cecilia 7th Grade

"MONEY MATTERS™ is a work of literacy and financial excellence."

-Abby Ruehlmann
Ursuline Academy 10th Grade

"What a great and timely resource for young people. No one and no course prepared me for the financial issues I'd face in the NFL; I wish I had this book when signing to the league."

-Lonie Paxton #66
Denver Broncos 3-time Super Bowl Champion

"The World of Pro Wrestling is a crazy world; none of us are prepared for or taught how to manage and make our money work for us. MONEY MATTERS™, wow what a book!"

-Matt Anoa'i, aka ROSEY
Former WWE Star

"...the concrete life examples, factual information, and activities in this book will help adolescents plan their financial future."

-Jessie Butash
Woonsocket Middle School Counselor

Order Information

Teen Response, Inc.
PO BOX 9555
Cincinnati, OH 45209-0555
www.teenresponse.org
www.mymoneymatters.us
www.mymoneymatters.biz

For contact information: Email jkeuffer@consultant.com

MONEY MATTERS™
By calling:

(513) 827-9096

Other Stuff

By
John R. Keuffer, III
Richard Carey
Kathy Garrison

DARE TO FAIL: STRIVE TO SUCCEED

www.p-t-w.com

Acknowledgements

We thank Jesus Christ our Lord and Savior; through him all things are possible.

John Keuffer

I would like to thank Robert & Kim Kiyosaki, Sharon Lechter and Zig Ziglar as they have been tremendous motivators and supporters over the years. Thanks to our good friends at Woonsocket Middle School; Jessie Butash.

Richard Carey

I would like to thank Bill and Suzy Goldberg along with Louis, Beth and Murray Guttman. Their support and wisdom has helped me over the years to become very successful in business.

Kathy Garrison

I would like to thank my sisters Pam, Patty, Debbie, Missy (and my deceased sister Joyce) for being my constant support, encouragement and their belief in my quest to make a difference.

Dedication

John R. Keuffer, III
This book is dedicated to my loving wife Kendra and my bonus daughter Hannah. I wish to recognize my parents John & Jaynee Keuffer. I'd also like to dedicate this to my sister Jaynee Behrens and her husband Mickey, Jenna-Lea and Mia Behrens. Of special note: My departed Grandmother Betty Madden whom I miss very much.

Richard Carey
I would like to dedicate this book to my children: Jerel, Cayla and Ceana. May you always reach for the top in all your endeavors. Don't Settle! Be a finisher!

Kathy Garrison
I would like to dedicate my involvement in writing this book to my husband, Jim who has always been and continues to be the "wind beneath my wings". To my children Chris and Steve and my grandchildren John, Nyssa, Kasia and Jay who inspire me every day.

Mark Wooten
I would like to dedicate my involvement in this book to my wife Emma who has been a blessing in my Life. My son's Mark and Ricky and grandchildren; Mark. Jr., Cameron, Tyler and Alivea who are a great joy in my Life.

Jim Beck
I would like to dedicate my involvement in this book to the Middle School Students at John P. Parker School in Madisonville, Ohio.

D.J. Sutton, II
I would like to dedicate this book to my parents, sister and my children; Marvin and Keegan.

Contents

BIG CITY
And the
Small Village

Once there was a King in a Big City who issued a decree to have a neighboring village destroyed. The only thing that could save the village was if one of the village people went to the Big City and won a debate with the King.

Later that night, all the village people gathered to see who would go to the Big City and debate the King in hopes of saving the village.

No one volunteered! Suddenly a small hand went up in the back and it was the town fool; also known as the village idiot. Since no one else would volunteer to debate against the King, they had no choice but to send the village idiot. He packed himself a brown bag lunch and was off to the Big City.

Arriving at the Big City, he saw the King sitting way up on a pedestal surrounded by all of his officials and people of the city.

The village idiot made his way to the King and the debate was on. Back in those days, debates were silent. People used only gestures or body language to debate. The King greeted the town fool, motioning with his right hand making a big circle from left to right (stating the whole village must go). The town fool points to the ground firmly (stating we're staying right here).

The King then shows three fingers (representing the Trinity: Father, Son and Holy Ghost). The town fool shows one finger (stating they're all one). The King sensing defeat takes a step back, puts his hands on his chin and pauses. He then turns around and grabs a tray full of bread and wine (representing the Lord's Supper and Holy Sacrament). He offers it to the village idiot. The village idiot rejects it and reaches into his own brown bag and pulls out a bright shiny apple (showing an act of rebellion and the sin committed by Adam and Eve). He takes a hearty bite of the apple and the debate was over.

The King said he'll spare the village! He sent the village idiot on his way. The officials looking puzzled by what had taken place and looked to the King for some answers.

The King stated that was the wisest man I've ever met. I told him "God was all around us, and he said God was right here! I then showed him three fingers representing Father, Son and Holy Ghost and He said they are all one. I offered him bread and wine representing a peace offering of the broken body of Christ and he pulls out an apple showing the fall of many through disobedience. He was the wisest man I've ever met!" The King continued to state "No harm shall come to their village."

The town fool returned to the village skipping down the road. The people see him and start running toward him. He shouts, "The village is saved!" One of the people shouted "What happened?"

The village idiot said, "Well, as soon as I got there, the King said 'the whole village must go!' and I said 'we're staying right here!'. Then he said, 'we have three days to leave' and I said 'Ain't one of us moving!' He then offered me some bread and wine and I rejected it. I pulled out my apple to show him that I had lunch too!

This is a classic tale of miscommunication. Throughout this book we want to communicate clearly—if you don't understand, ask for help and learn these topics with a friend or family member to make them more fun and challenging.

INTRODUCTION

Why is financial literacy important to you? Let's face it, we all like money. They call it cold and hard. Well the last time we felt a dollar it was neither cold nor hard—in fact, we thought it felt good.

Some will tell you, "Money is the root of all evil!" This is not correct; they have incorrectly quoted the Bible. What it really says in 1 Timothy 6:10 is *"For the love of money is the root of all evil"*.

Money is neither good nor evil. It is simply a neutral object; nothing more than a tool. Is a hammer good or evil? The object itself is neither good nor evil—if it truly is a tool, then only the person using the tool can be good or evil.

A hammer used to hit someone is still a neutral object, but the act of hitting someone with the hammer would be evil.

This Bible verse simply cautions mankind and reminds us that we are commanded not to place other gods before GOD. If we allow ourselves to worship at the altar of a dollar, then the dollar becomes our god in place of the one true Lord. So if we <u>love</u> money, then it becomes the root of our evil as it becomes a god we are worshipping in violation of God's law.

Deuteronomy 5: 6-21 states, "You shall have no other gods before me. You shall not make for yourself an idol, whether in the form of anything that is in heaven above, or that is on the earth beneath, or that is in the water under the earth. You shall not bow down to them or worship them…"

So the next time you hear someone tell you that "money is the root of all evil" you can now politely "school" them.

Why is it so important to become financially literate? Because most of your adult decisions and options in life will center on money. You will inevitably spend a significant amount of time discussing money--the lack of, how to get more and what to do with it once you've got it.

Why is money so important? Here are a couple of stories...

A Little Story about a Boy Named Abe:

There was a boy named Abe. His parents had very little money coming in. So Abe decided to work hard and pay for college himself. He became a lawyer. He learned how to make his money grow. Eventually, he got an important job and stayed wealthy. That boy was Abraham Lincoln.

Another Little Story about another Boy Named George:

A boy named George was also poor. His parents put him in an orphanage. He became an athlete and made even more money than the President of the United States. But he didn't know how to keep that money. Pretty soon, there wasn't much left. George's middle name was Herman, but everyone called him Babe - Babe Ruth.

The lessons in these stories are the same. **YOU** control what happens to the money in your life—your money will work, whether it's for you or someone else remains to be determined by the choices you make with it.

Money will be a significant issue for you for the rest of your life. A lot of your choices will be based upon whether or not you have money, have enough, or have resources to get more. This book is presented to help give you a head start and a new way of seeing money and how it can work for you.

To help you on your journey and ensure that you get all of the insight possible, our friends Saver Sam and Penny Pete will be there to help guide you.

Saver Sam likes to provide historical information on money, currency and it's relevance in our history, while Penny Pete likes to challenge people and present new ideas.

COME JOIN US AND LET'S LEARN ABOUT MONEY!

Saver Sam

Money Fact!

The history of money spans thousands of years. Numismatics is the scientific study of money and its history in all its varied forms.

Many items have been used as commodity money such as naturally scarce precious metals, conch shells, barley, beads etc., as well as many other things that are thought of as having value.

Modern money (and most ancient money) is essentially a token — in other words, an abstraction. Paper currency is perhaps the most common type of physical money today. However, objects of gold or silver present many of money's essential properties. The term Price system is sometimes used to refer to methods using commodity valuation or money accounting systems.

Claudius II Coin

1

WHAT IS MONEY

> **"I have enough money to last me the rest of my life, unless I buy something."**
> **-Jackie Mason (1934 -)**

Can you tell us what this is a picture of? Go ahead and take a good long, hard look at it and tell us what you see when you look at this picture? What does this picture mean to you when you look at it? If you have a dollar in your pocket, take it out and take a good hard look at the real deal.

Is it a dollar bill? Yes. Is it legal tender? Yes. Is it a paper representation of one hundred pennies or four quarters, or ten dimes or twenty nickels? Yes. All of those are correct—but what we are asking is "what do you see when you look at a dollar bill; especially a dollar bill that is in your pocket or wallet?"

When you see a dollar bill, especially one that is in your hand, wallet or pocket; what do you think of? What does a dollar mean to you? Before we can begin teaching you anything about money, we have to learn how you view money.

So what is it you think of when looking at that dollar bill on the previous page or a dollar in your pocket?

_____

_____

_____

_____

_____

_____

_____

We bet some of your answers included: "It's one hundred pennies; it's cold, hard cash; it's a bag of chips; a bottle of soft drink or a candy bar!

WRONG! IT'S AN EMPLOYEE!

That is old thinking and we have to get you to step in to new thinking. Every dollar in your hand, wallet or pocket is an **<u>EMPLOYEE!</u>** That dollar has one task in its life and that is to work for someone. That dollar is either working for you or it's working for someone else. Check your answer to the questions below:

Who is that dollar working for when you go in to a store and buy a bag of chips?   _ Grocery Store Owner   __ Me

Who is your dollar working for when you go to a movie theater?
     _ Movie Theater Owner   __ Me

Who is your dollar working for when you buy that new CD?
     _ Record Company   __ Me

Who is your dollar working for when you buy that football trading card?   _ Trading Card Company __ Me

If you checked "ME" for any of these questions, you are WRONG!

When your dollar goes to purchase those items, your dollar becomes an employee for those companies. The convenient store owner thanks you. The Trading Card Company and the Pro Athlete both thank you.

You have to start thinking of yourself as a company. You are (Fill In Your Name)_____, Inc. Each dollar in your wallet or pocket is an Employee of (Fill In Your Name)_____, Inc.

Now that you are (Fill In Your Name)_____ Inc. How does it feel to be the BOSS? As the Boss, how will you manage your employees (money)?

If your money is like your employee, would it be okay for your employees (money) to work for another company? __ Yes __ No

If your money is like your employee; would it be okay for your employees (money) to sit around and take a break each day? __ Yes __ No

It's obvious you wouldn't let your employees go work for another company and you sure wouldn't let them take a break all day. On the contrary, you want your employees working for whom? **YOU**, that's who! And if they are sitting around taking a break all day, they aren't helping you make money are they?

Saver Sam

Money Fact!

Money is anything that is generally accepted as payment for goods and services and repayment of debts. The main uses of money are as a medium of exchange, a unit of account, and a store of value. The word "money" is believed to originate from a temple of Hera, located on Capitoline, one of Rome's seven hills. In the ancient world Hera was often associated with money. The temple of Juno Moneta at Rome was the place where the mint of Ancient Rome was located.

Money is generally considered to have the following characteristics, which are summed up in a rhyme found in older economics textbooks: "Money is a matter of four functions, a medium, a measure, a standard, a store." That is, money functions as a medium of exchange, a unit of account, a standard of deferred payment, and a store of value.

*Resource: Wikipedia

2

HOW MUCH IS RICH?

"Money is plentiful for those who understand the simple laws which govern its acquisition."
-George Clason (1874 - 1957)

CONGRATULATIONS! YOU JUST WON $1 MILLION DOLLARS! Now what?

Let's pretend for a moment that you just hit the lottery and won $1 million dollars! That would be great, wouldn't it? Imagine that photo above is really a $1 million dollar bill and it is all yours!

What are you going to do now? From the list below place a check mark next to the things you are going to do now with your million dollars—happy spending!

HOUSE and LOCATION:

3 bedroom/2 bath house in California   ___
3 bedroom/2bath condo in New York City   ___

VEHICLE:

Newest Model BMW Sports Car   ___
Newest Model Cadillac Escalade   ___
Newest Model Porsche Sports Car   ___

MOM & DAD:

Buy Mom/Dad/Grandparents a New Home   ___
Buy Mom/Dad/Grandparents a New Car   ___

TRAVEL:

Will travel Europe for 30 days of vacation   ___
Will travel the USA for 30 days of vacation   ___
Will travel South America for 30 days of vacation   ___

Car Additions:

Top of the line Spinners   ___
Top of the line Sound System   ___
DVD/TV/Game System Hook Up   ___

HOUSE ADDITIONS:

Top of the line in-ground pool   ___
3-car garage   ___
Theater Room fully loaded   ___
Family Fun Room fully loaded   ___

EMPLOYMENT:

Will you work or quit your job? (Circle one)   WORK   QUIT

ENTOURAGE:

Will you do all of this alone or will you bring your crew?
    ALONE   CREW

How many are in your crew?   _____

That was a lot of fun, wasn't it? We bet you are smiling from ear to ear thinking about how great all of that stuff would be to have! Now let's take a look at how much money you have left. Sorry, did we forget to tell you that you had to pay for all of this? Ooops!

Mark an 'x' next to your answers from the previous pages, write the corresponding dollar amount on the blank line provided, and then add it all up.

HOUSE and LOCATION:
3 bedroom/2 bath house in California	$675,000.00	_____
3 bedroom/2bath condo in New York City	$500,000.00	_____

VEHICLE:
Newest Model BMW Sports Car	$ 75,000.00	_____
Newest Model Cadillac Escalade	$ 65,000.00	_____
Newest Model Porsche Sports Car	$ 85,000.00	_____

MOM & DAD:
Buy Mom/Dad/Grandparents a New Home	$250,000.00	_____
Buy Mom/Dad/Grandparents a New Car	$ 35,000.00	_____

TRAVEL:
Will travel Europe for 30 days of vacation	$ 30,000.00	_____
Will travel the USA for 30 days of vacation	$ 35,000.00	_____
Will travel South America for 30 days of vacation	$ 25,000.00	_____

Car Additions:
Top of the line Spinners	$ 20,000.00	_____
Top of the line Sound System	$ 25,000.00	_____
DVD/TV/Game System Hook Up	$ 15,000.00	_____

HOUSE ADDITIONS:
Top of the line in-ground pool	$ 40,000.00	_____
3-car garage	$100,000.00	_____
Theater Room fully loaded	$ 25,000.00	_____
Family Fun Room fully loaded	$ 25,000.00	_____

EMPLOYMENT:
Work	DEDUCT -	$ 35,000.00	_____
Quit	ADD+	$ 35,000.00	_____

TOTAL _____

ENTOURAGE:
Alone	multiply x 1	_____
If you have a crew, multiply the TOTAL by number in your crew x __		_____

HOW MUCH MONEY IS LEFT? _____

Where did all of your money go? We bet you spent almost all of it. Even if you hadn't spent the full million dollars; you have to ask whether or not having $1 million dollars makes you rich or not?

The average life expectancy in the U.S. is 77 years of age. If you are 15 at the time of reading this book, you are expected to live another 62 years. If you were to spread your million dollars out over your expected life span, you would only have $16,129.03 per year to live on. Can't quite retire on that now can you?

Check the chart below: (To determine other ages; Subtract your age from 77 and divide $1,000,000 by that number and you will see how much per year you would have to live on if you tried to make that $1million last)

Age	Per Year Income
11	$15,151.51
12	$15,384.61
13	$15,625.00
14	$15,873.01
16	$16,393.44
17	$16,666.66
18	$16,949.15
19	$17,241.37
20	$17,543.85

Can we agree that simply having $1 million dollars does not allow us to do everything we thought we could do and for the rest of our lives? Having an understanding about the value of money is very important. If you don't understand a dollar, you will never understand a million dollars.

Having $1 million dollars won't allow you to retire if you are a teenager; but it will give you options; options that others don't have.

THE PENNY PETE CHALLENGE!

Would you rather have $1,000,000 dollars right now in your hands or one penny that would double in value each day for 30 days?

Select One: ____ $1,000,000   ____.01¢ That Doubles

Let's see if you made a good choice or not.

Week 1		
Day No.	Pay for that Day	Total Amount
1	.01	.01
2	.02	.03
3	.04	.07
4	.08	.15
5	.16	.31
6	.32	.63
7	.64	**1.27**

One week has gone by, how are you feeling about your choice to either take the penny or the $1,000,000? You only have $1.27 thus far!

Are you still confident in your choice? __ Yes __ No

Week 2		
Day No.	Pay for that Day	Total Amount
8	1.28	2.55
9	2.56	5.11
10	5.12	10.23
11	10.24	20.47
12	20.48	40.95
13	40.96	81.91
14	81.92	**163.83**

It's starting to pick up a little, how are you feeling so far? It's not too late to change your mind. Are you sticking with your original decision or are you going to move ahead? You have $163.83 if you chose the penny option.

Week 3		
Day No.	Pay for that Day	Total Amount
15	163.84	327.67
16	327.68	655.35
17	655.36	1,310.71
18	1 310.72	2, 621.43
19	2 621.44	5, 242.87
20	5 242.88	10, 485.75
21	10 485.76	**20, 971.51**

It's up to $20,971.51 in 21 days; are you still sticking to your original choice? _____ Yes _____ No

Week 4		
Day No.	Pay for that Day	Total Amount
22	20 971.51	41, 943.03
23	41 943.04	83, 886.07
24	83 886.08	167 ,772.15
25	167 772.16	335, 544.31
26	335 544.32	671, 088.63
27	671 088.64	1, 342, 177.27
28	1 342 177.28	**2, 684, 354.55**

Oh No! If you chose the $1,000,000 offer you really missed out. In just 28 days the penny has gone from .01 to $2,684,354.55!!

But that's not it! We still have two more days!

FINAL TWO DAYS		
Day No.	Pay for that Day	Total Amount
29	2 684 354.56	5, 368 ,709.11
30	5 368 709.12	**10, 737, 418.23**

How did you do? Did you stay with your original choice or change it?

"AND YOU THOUGHT THOSE PENNIES WERE USELESS!"

Saver Sam

Money Fact!

The history of the dollar in North America pre-dates US independence. Even before the Declaration of Independence, the Continental Congress had authorized the issuance of dollar denominated coins and currency, since the term 'dollar' was in common usage referring to Spanish colonial 8 real coins or "Spanish Milled Dollars". Though several monetary systems were proposed for the early republic, the dollar was approved by Congress in a largely symbolic resolution on 8 August 1786.

After passage of the Constitution was secured, the government turned its attention to monetary issues again in the early 1790s under the leadership of Alexander Hamilton, the Secretary of the Treasury at the time. Congress acted on Hamilton's recommendations in the Coinage Act of 1792, which established the Dollar as the basic unit of account for the United States

*Resource: Wikipedia

3

BUT I'M GONNA BE A STAR BABY!

"Ever notice how it's a penny for your thoughts, yet you put in your two cents? Someone is making a penny on the deal!"
-Stephen Wright (1955 -)

You might be thinking in your mind, "I don't need to worry about all of this; I'm going to be a star (athlete, singer, rapper)!" Listen closely, **WE ARE NOT TRYING TO STEAL YOUR DREAMS!** We just want you to understand that you should be prepared for anything and have options.

Since being a star is one of your aspirations, let's take a look at what it might be like if you considered being in the NFL.

In order to even be considered for the NFL, you have to first get in to college. Out of all the high schools in the United States over 100,000 students are college eligible athletes for football.

There are 119 Division I NCAA Colleges; they may only pick up 10 eligible students (if that many) per College-so out of the 100,000 eligible student athletes, approximately 1,200 students will receive a full or partial scholarship.

So let's assume you were one of those 1,200 students selected. Now you have to make it through College, at least until your junior year before you can be draft eligible.

If you make it that far, there are only 32 NFL Teams carrying 55 members per team, totaling 1,760 players. Each year over 6,000 student-athletes are eligible for the Draft from Division I schools alone. Again, the key word is eligible; doesn't mean they are all wanted. If we were to factor in Division II and III; we would be looking at tens of thousands.

If the NFL can only carry 1,760 players—less than 1% will be called to try out with an NFL team.

Of course we understand that you are special and your talents aren't like anyone else in the league-so let's assume you make it to the NFL. What is the average career life for an NFL Player? It's 3 ½ years!

How many of the people on a team do you think make top dollar? Not many. Only 3-4 of the players are the top paid players on a team; that is, the ones who make multi-year deals worth multi millions. Most players are receiving near the league minimum. In 2000, the NFL Players Association reported that the average salary was $193,000 per season for players.

In 2008, the NFL Players Association reported the average salary as being $1.1 million dollars. That is the average—so that means some are making more and some are making less.

As we learned before, $1 million is not enough to retire on and expect to live a high quality lifestyle until you are in your seventies.

Another interesting statistic the NFL Players Association mentions is that players with degrees earn 20-30% more than players without degrees. They offer no concrete evidence as to why this happens, but they suspect it's because those players show qualities of concentration, intelligence and mental discipline which help to propel them off the field as well.

But let's face it; if you're dumb with $10, you will be dumb with $10 million.

Ask yourself this question: why do so many former players in the NFL have to take on other jobs after their playing days? Quite simply, they have to work because as their pay increased so did their standard of living-then when they stopped playing and getting paid the large amount of money, they needed an income source to help maintain that lifestyle or any lifestyle.

Here is a little inside information about contracts in the NFL. The only money that is guaranteed in your contract is the signing bonus money. The signing bonus is the upfront money they give you when signing a contract. The NFL can cut you (release you) and not pay you any of the money in the contract.

How can that be? Let's say you made it all the way and were drafted in the NFL. They offer you a 5 year/$10 million dollar contract with a $1 million signing bonus.

You make it through camp, if you are lucky, and you play one season. At the end of that season they decided it just didn't work out and they want to cut you. How much will you make for that one year?

You will receive the $1 million for the signing bonus and you will receive $2 million for the first year you played. So your total take will be $3 million for your membership in the NFL club. I forgot to mention that your agent will be taking 3% of your take for representing you.

Is $3 million enough to retire on at the age of 21? NO! We could go in to injuries and all sorts of things with the NFL. The bottom line: Have a back up plan!

Now if you are sitting there and you say, "That's okay, I want to be an American Idol." Well, just look up the stats on Fantasia Barrino who won in 2004. There is a long list of famous people who have filed for bankruptcy after claiming fame and fortune. Why? Again, if you are stupid with $10, you will be stupid with $10 million. Did you know that songwriters only make .91 cents for each album sold?

Always, have a back up plan! Understanding money and finance is always a good back up plan.

To see list of famous bankruptcies:
http://rjabankruptcy.com/articles/famousindividuals.html

Saver Sam

Money Fact!

The word "dollar" is derived from Low Saxon "daler", an abbreviation of "Joachimsdaler" – (coin) from Joachimsthal (St. Joachim's Valley, now Jáchymov, Bohemia, then part of the Holy Roman Empire, now part of the Czech Republic – so called because it was minted from 1519 onwards using silver extracted from a mine which had opened in 1516 near Joachimstal, a town in the Ore Mountains of northwestern Bohemia. The term "dollar" was widely used in reference to a Spanish coin at the time it was adopted by the United States. Because prices of gold and silver in the open marketplace vary independently, the production of coins of full intrinsic worth under any ratio will nearly always result in the melting of either all silver coins or all gold coins. In the early 1800s, gold rose in relation to silver, resulting in the removal from commerce of nearly all gold coins, and their subsequent melting. Therefore, in 1834, the 15:1 ratio was changed to a 16:1 ratio by reducing the weight of the nation's gold coinage. This created a new U.S. dollar that was backed by 1.50 g (23.22 grains) of gold.

*Resource: Wikipedia

4

HOW IS MONEY MADE?

Ever wonder about those people who spend $2 apiece on those little bottles of Evian water? Try spelling Evian backward."
- George Carlin (1937 – 2008)

Despite the opinion of most youth; money does not grow on a tree and your parents aren't made of it.

Recently one of our groups' young daughters was out shopping with a friend and when they realized they were out of money, they devised a plan. "I know what we can do." said the one girl to the other. "Let's get this card my dad has. When he puts it in to this machine, money just comes out!," she exclaimed.

She honestly thought her dad had this magical card that allowed him to print money any time he needed it. She didn't understand that this was a Bank Card and that he could only take out as much money as he had put in the bank.

So let's make sure we are all on the same page here and we have at least this understanding:

1) Money does not grow on trees; and,

2) Your parents are made of flesh and blood, not money; and,

3) There is no such thing as a magical card that allows you or anyone else to print money.

What are some of the ways you think money is earned?

_____

_____

_____

_____

_____

_____

_____

_____

_____

_____

_____

_____

_____

_____

_____

_____

_____

_____

_____

_____

_____

_____

FOUR SQUARE

Have you ever played '*four square*' in the playground? You know, the game where four people each stand in a box and hits a rubber ball to the other squares trying to get the other person to miss.

Much like the design of the 'four square' box, you can diagram how people can earn money.

TIME FOR MONEY These are the Sweat Laborers	**TIME IS MONEY** These people have flexibility
PAID WORKER	FINANCIER
SELF EMPLOYED	BUSINESS OWNER

On one side you have *PAID WORKER* and the *SELF EMPLOYED*, while on the other side you have *FINANCIER* and *BUSINESS OWNER*.

So the ways to make money in life are by either being a Paid Worker, Self Employed, Financier, or Business Owner.

On one side of the 'four square' you have the people who have to 'sweat', meaning they have to work and exchange their time for money.

TIME FOR MONEY These are the Sweat Laborers
PAID WORKER
SELF EMPLOYED

On the other side of the 'four square' you have people who realize time is money and they make money whether they are at work or not.

TIME IS MONEY These people have flexibility
FINANCIER
BUSINESS OWNER

What side of the 'four square' are your Parents/Grandparents on?

_____ Time For Money   _____ Time Is Money

TIME FOR MONEY:

TIME FOR MONEY
These are the Sweat Laborers

PAID WORKER

SELF EMPLOYED

A **PAID WORKER** works for someone else and he trades his time for money. When you are a paid worker you work for someone else who pays you based on the exchange of your time for their money.

As a Paid Worker you are limited by the amount the business owner is willing to pay per hour of time and the amount of time he is willing to pay for. So if the owner is only willing to pay $10/hour for 40 hours per week; you can only make $400 per week that means you can only make how much per year?

$400 per week @ 52 weeks per year = $_____/year

That's not enough to retire on or to have the things you would enjoy having in life, is it?

What are some examples of a Paid Worker? _____
_____
_____

| **TIME FOR MONEY** |
| These are the Sweat Laborers |
| PAID WORKER |
| **SELF EMPLOYED** |

A **SELF EMPLOYED** person is a person who also trades time for money. You may know a few self-employed people. These people are the jack's of all trades—they have to run everything and be all things in order to make money.

If they aren't working, they aren't making money. They have to keep their books, do the work, find the customers, market the business—phew; it's tiring just typing all of that stuff!

If a self employed person decides to not work today he will not be making any money. Everything he does relies heavily on their involvement or input. For example—a doctor in private practice makes money by seeing patients. If that doctor decides to take the day off to play golf, he isn't seeing any patients and therefore no one is making a payment to the doctor for the visit.

Even if this doctor charges $200 an hour and works eight hours per day and 5 days per week for one year; how much is the maximum he can earn in a year?

$200/hour @ 8 hours/day @ 5 days/week @ 52 weeks = $_____
It's a lot—but is it enough to make him/her *RICH*?

TIME IS MONEY:

TIME IS MONEY   These people have flexibility
FINANCIER
BUSINESS OWNER

A *FINANCIER* (pronounced; fin-an-cier) is somebody who is skilled in finance and invests his or her money in financial matters. A Financier could invest in business ideas, stocks, real estate or other financial investment opportunities.

What is important for the Financier is how much will he or she make back from their investment? They focus on a term called, ROI; Return On Investment. He wants to know, "What is my profit from an investment as a percentage of the amount invested?

A Financier invests in a 12-Unit Apartment House that is for sale in the amount of $350,000, making a down payment of $50,000 cash and borrowing $300,000 from the bank. After receiving the monthly rents, paying loan and all operating costs the Financier has a Net monthly Cashflow of $1,200. What is his ROI?

Return On Investment (ROI): (Your monthly Cashflow x 12 months)/ Your Down Payment.

Monthly Cashflow Profit: $_____ (Cashflow) x 12 months =
$_____ (A)
$_____ (A)/$_____ Down Payment = _____%

The Financier is looking at using their money to make it grow and work for them; helping them to increase their initial investment.

See if you can figure out the ROI on this deal:

4-Unit Commercial Property For Sale at $250,000.00. The down payment is $25,000.00 leaving a mortgage of $225,000.00. You will receive a monthly Cashflow of $500.00. What is the ROI % for this potential investment?

_____
_____
_____
_____
_____
_____
_____
_____
_____
_____
_____
_____
_____
_____
_____
_____

| TIME IS MONEY |
| These people have flexibility |
| FINANCIER |
| **BUSINESS OWNER** |

A ***BUSINESS OWNER*** is a person or other organization that buys and sells goods, makes products, or provides services. An example of a Business Owner is Ray Kroc (if you've ever eaten at McDonald's, you know Ray's work).

A Business Owner is someone or a group of people who form a company or take over a company and oversee its operations. Another example of a Business Owner is the famous Malouf Family. They own the Sacramento Kings, The Palms Hotel and Casino in Vegas.

There are many examples of various people who are Business Owners from all walks of life; such as, the Earnhardt family of NASCAR fame, Country legend Dolly Parton and many others.

These people establish or purchase a product, produce it or provide a service to others who are willing to pay for such services.

THE PENNY PETE CHALLENGE!

CLASSIFY THE JOB WITH THE FOUR SQUARE CATEGORY!

For Each Job Title, write down the corresponding letter for each of the **'four square'** sections to determine what category each job falls under.

Example: Teacher <u>PW</u>   Paid Worker

PW= Paid Worker   **S** = Self Employed
F= Financier   **BO**= Business Owner

1. Police Officer   ——

2. NBA Player   ——

3. Lawyer   ——

4. Landlord   ——

5. Stock Broker   ——

6. Lawn Care   ——

7. Banker   ——

8. NFL Player   ——

9. NFL Commissioner   ——

10. TV News Anchor   ——

11. Music Artist   ——

12. Tutor   ——

13. Auto Mechanic   ——

14. McDonalds Owner   ——

15. McDonald's Worker   ——

Saver Sam

Money Fact!

In 1853, the weights of US silver coins (except, interestingly, the dollar itself, which was rarely used) were reduced. This had the effect of placing the nation effectively (although not officially) on the gold standard. The retained weight in the dollar coin was a nod to bimetallism, although it had the effect of further driving the silver dollar coin from commerce.

With the enactment (1863) of the National Banking Act during the American Civil War and its later versions that taxed states' bonds and currency out of existence, the dollar became the sole currency of the United States and remains so today.

In 1878, the Bland-Allison Act was enacted to provide for freer coinage of silver. This act required the government to purchase between $2 million and $4 million worth of silver bullion each month at market prices and to coin it into silver dollars. This was, in effect, a subsidy for politically influential silver producers.

*Resource: Wikipedia

5

SWEAT
WORK
OR
SMART WORK

"I've got all the money I'll ever need if I die by four o'clock this afternoon."
- Henny Youngman (1906 – 1998)

In the last chapter we talked about the 'Four Square' concept and showed you the four ways people can earn money. On the left side you had those who traded their time for money while on the right side we had the people who make money no matter what their time investment is.

What are some ways you can <u>earn</u> money?

____ Lawn Mowing   ____ Paper Route   ____ Taking Trash
____ Recycling   ____ Cutting Hair   ____ Gardening
____ Tutoring   ____ Running Errands   ____ Cleaning
____ Shoveling Snow

Can you think of any other ways? _____

_____

_____

_____

_____

_____

Despite what you may think, there are many ways to earn money. Almost everyone has to start out as a PAID WORKER. Most of us have to start at the bottom and trade our time for someone else's money.

It's possible that there are some people in the world that jumped straight to the FINANCIER or BUSINESS OWNER side; but for the great majority of us, we had to start at the bottom and work our way up.

There is nothing wrong with starting this way. Starting out as a Paid Worker allows you an opportunity to gain valuable knowledge and lessons in the working world. Use this as an opportunity to learn.

Looking at the list on page 41, how can you take some of the earning opportunities and make them in to business opportunities where you are earning money working but doing it smarter?

Example: At some point in our lives most people have cut the grass whether for their own parents or for a neighbor. Selling your services to a neighbor to cut their grass would be considered working as a

___ Paid Worker ___ Self-Employed ___ Financier ___ Business Owner

Which did you check and why?_____

_____
_____
_____
_____
_____
_____
_____
_____

What if you decided to get a few grass cutting contracts with 5 neighbors? Each neighbor agrees to pay you $20 per lawn per week in return for you cutting their grass. Selling your services to cut the grass of several neighbor's yards would be considered working as a:

___ Paid Worker ___ Self-Employed ___ Financier ___ Business Owner

Which did you check that and why? _____

_____

_____

_____

_____

_____

_____

What if you had the same 5 neighbors contracted to cut their grass for $20 each yard and you went and found a friend or two and offered them $10 for cutting each yard each week and you collected the $10 profit. You get the contracts and provide the equipment for them to use to cut the grass along with the oil and gas needed for the mower. Which 'four square' box would you fall under?

___ Paid Worker ___ Self-Employed ___ Financier ___ Business Owner

Which did you check and why? _____

_____

_____

_____

_____

_____

_____

_____

Now let's suppose you didn't want to do any of those things. You don't want to cut the grass, get the contracts or supervise the people doing any of those things; but you have some money that you'd like to use to earn more money.

Your friend approaches you and he has contracts for those 5 same yards at $20 each year, but he doesn't own a lawnmower and doesn't have money for oil and gas to operate the lawnmower. You offer your friend the money that he needs to purchase a lawnmower and some money to get oil and gas. In return, your friend will pay you $5 per yard for the entire summer.

Which 'four square' box would you fall under?

___ Paid Worker ___ Self-Employed ___ Financier ___ Business Owner

Which did you check and why? _____
_____
_____
_____
_____
_____
_____
_____
_____
_____
_____

ANSWER KEY: PW, S, BO, F

The idea is not to discuss or point anything out as good or bad; the idea is to start to get you to think outside of the box with regards to ways of making money and not just as a Paid Worker, Self-Employed, Financier or Business Owner.

As a kid you have a lot of possibilities to discover ways to earn. Fortunately for you as a kid you don't have all of the hang ups most adults have and the fears of failure.

Taking an idea like cutting the grass or being a barber and looking at the income potentials and possibilities is the challenge for you. Today, many kids cut each others hair and take a fee for it. Cutting hair is a fine profession; but what if you set up a business and recruit other barbers who need a place to cut hair and the equipment to set up shop in your business. They would then pay you rent for the space? That simple act takes you from being a Paid Worker to now being a Business Owner and offers you other income earning potential without you having to do all of the work.

That is called **SMART WORK** and not **SWEAT WORK.**

Saver Sam

Money Fact!

The National Monetary Commission

A particularly severe panic in 1907 provided the motivation for renewed demands for banking and currency reform. The following year Congress enacted the Aldrich-Vreeland Act which provided for an emergency currency and established the National Monetary Commission to study banking and currency reform.

The chief of the bipartisan National Monetary Commission was financial expert and Senate Republican leader Nelson Aldrich. Aldrich set up two commissions—one to study the American Monetary system in depth and the other, headed by Aldrich himself, to study the European central-banking systems and report on them. Aldrich went to Europe opposed to centralized banking, but after viewing Germany's banking system, he came away believing that a centralized bank was better than the government-issued bond system that he had previously supported.

*Resource: Wikipedia

6

SIX FIRST AID CURES FOR A SKINNY WALLET!

"Somebody said to me, 'but the Beatles were anti-materialistic.' That's a huge myth. John and I literally used to sit down and say, 'Now, let's write a swimming pool.'
- Paul McCartney (1942 -)

START FEEDING YOUR WALLET:

If you had ten dollars and we told you to take one dollar and put it in your wallet and not spend it and every time you got money you should take 1/10 of it and put in your wallet without spending, what would happen over time?

Eventually you would start to increase the value and amount of money you had saved up in your wallet. Over time that wallet would start to feel heavier and with time you will have the satisfaction of having been diligent in your efforts..

Far too often we get money and pay other people first. Why should you work hard to earn money only to give it to someone else?

We all work too hard; and many of us, especially your parents and grandparents work each day just to pay the car dealer, the banker, the cable company, taxes to the government, the credit card companies and many others to whom they owe money. Shouldn't we get paid something first?

To start fattening your wallet, take out 10% of all you earn and pay yourself first. You can use the other 70% to buy whatever you want or need, but consistently keeping 10% consistently and putting that away as savings is not an easy task, after you've done it enough, it will become a rewarding habit.

<u>Task</u>: start saving 10% of all your money for one month.

ESTABLISH A BUDGET AND CONTROL YOUR EXPENSES:

Your parents might say, "How can I save 10% when I can barely get by on what I make right now?" Let's face it; we all want more than we can afford to buy. No matter how much money we have, we still have things we'd like to buy but can't afford.

There is a saying, "As your income increases so do your expenses." Most people try to find more things to buy when they have more money. Budgeting will help you keep track of where your money is going; it will also show you places where you might be wasting money. The tedious nature of writing down every single penny you spend will typically help you eliminate some minor spending. You may find that writing down a soft drink or bag of chips every day will become tedious and therefore you will learn that perhaps you don't need those things.

"Why would I want to write everything down? That will just make me feel like a slave." you might ask.

You may already be a slave in some form or fashion. When you owe money to other people or when you don't have options in life because of the lack of money or proper management of money, you certainly can be a slave to the people you owe money to and a slave to not being able to enjoy the options having money can provide.

Ultimately, you are the one who will set your budget. You will determine if enjoying short-term pleasures outweighs the enjoyment of future financial independence.

Task: Write down in a notebook every penny you spend for one week.

Extra Bonus Task: Ask your parents to do the same.

MAKE YOUR MONEY MULTIPLY:

It's time you start making your money work for you. Remember in Chapter 1 how we discussed every dollar you possess is an EMPLOYEE? Well, it's time to get those employees working and earning more money for you.

If the money you have been saving up sits in a bank account or a Certificate of Deposit, it can earn you anywhere from 1% to 10% interest per year, depending on the present interest rates and how much shopping around you do when researching this.

If you got an allowance or did some job weekly and earned $10 each week and you put 10% ($1.00) away in savings each week for one year, you would have saved $52. If you put the $52 in the bank you would make an additional .52cents to $5.20 per year in interest. It doesn't seem like a lot of course, but that is an example of how your money, your employees, can earn money for you.

Your true wealth is determined not by how much you can work to earn, but by how much your money can earn by working for you, whether you work or not. This is called *compounding* – when the return on your money earns more money. This is also known as *passive income* – money that comes in when you aren't working for it.

Let's take that same $52.00 you saved for one year and let's say you had it in the bank earning 5% interest for one year. You would have an additional $2.60 from interest making your new balance in the bank $54.60. If you decided to leave that money in the bank and continue to get 5% interest you would earn an additional $_____ and that would make your new balance $_____.

This is how to make your money multiply and fatten your wallet up-get your employees out there earning for you.

GUARD YOUR WALLET FROM LOSS:

With money comes a great temptation. Remember, if you are dumb with $1.00 you will more than likely be dumb with $1 million. It's important that as you start to fatten your wallet you stay smart and guard against schemes that will take your money. The ability to not lose what you have is a key to building wealth. Don't let your desires to make money fast control your decisions. Be extra careful of other people who try to help you invest **YOUR** money. The advice of people who do not regularly make their own money is usually worthless and risky. Seek the advice of successful people. Start building a core group of people around you who you can learn from.

PLAN FOR RETIREMENT:

"Retirement! But I'm only a teenager." Plan for it anyway and start working on it now. Life is short and that is a hard reality to grasp when you are young. You have to ask yourself, *Do you plan to work until you are in your 70's or would you like to retire while you are still young enough to enjoy it?*

Personally, retiring young while you can enjoy it sounds a lot more interesting. However, if you don't start working on that now, you won't have that opportunity.

Always put money aside that you will never touch.

INCREASE YOUR EARNING POTENTIAL:

Knowledge is your most valuable asset. There are many people who have twenty years of experience on a job when in all honesty, they have 1 year of experience repeated 20 times! If you want the opportunity to earn more, you must increase your knowledge and your skills. Increasing your knowledge has nothing to do with whether or not you go to college. College is not a guarantee for financial success-but knowledge is always an asset you can use more of.

You must start investing in yourself. Too often we spend too much money on what is outside of our heads: haircuts, glasses, teeth whitening, tans, etc. We need to spend less on the outside and start spending on putting things on the inside of our heads like knowledge!

"The Man who does not read good books has no advantage over the man who cannot read them."
-Mark Twain (1835 – 1910)

Saver Sam

Money Fact!

If the Native American tribe that accepted goods worth 60 guilders for the sale of Manhattan in 1626 had invested the money in Dutch Bank at 6.5% interest, compounded annually, then in 2005 their investment would be worth over $1 trillion US Dollars. That is more than the assessed value of the real estate in all five boroughs of New York City.

With a 6.0% interest however, the value of their investment today would have been around $100 billion.

Compound interest was once regarded as the worst kind of usury, and was severely condemned by Roman law, as well as the common laws of many other countries.

*Resource: Wikipedia

7

FIVE
LAWS
OF MONEY

"I finally know what distinguishes man from other beasts: financial worries."
- Pierre-Jules Renard (1864 - 1910)

#1   **Money will come in increasing quantity to anyone who puts no less than 10% of his earnings to create a savings for his future and the future of his family.**

What do you think this means? _____

_____

_____

_____

_____

#2   **Money works thoroughly and with satisfaction for a smart owner who treats it as an employee and finds it ways to earn profits.**

What do you think this means? _____

_____

_____

_____

_____

#3   **Money will cling for protection to the owner who invests it only under advice of successful people who understand how to wisely invest.**

What do you think this means? _____

_____

_____

_____

_____

#4   **Money will slip away from the owner who invests it in business or purposes which they are not familiar or not approved by those skilled in such investments.**

What do you think this means? _____

_____

_____

_____

_____

#5   **Money will run away from the owner who forces it to raise impossible earnings or who follows the advice of schemers and tricksters.**

What do you think this means? _____

_____

_____

_____

_____

An important lesson to learn is that just because you are paid a lot of money for a God-given talent does not mean you know how to "**make**" money.

The Five Laws of Money are there to help you understand that money is a tool that requires a wise owner. It is important in all aspects of your life to always seek the advice of someone who is smarter than yourself and more knowledgeable in areas you are not.

Your best friend, neighbor and even Mom or Dad aren't always the people whose advice you should take on money matters. Find someone who is successful and follow him and learn from him.

Saver Sam

Money Fact!

Central Banking in the US prior to the Federal Reserve:

The Federal Reserve System is the 3rd central banking system in US history. The First Bank of the US (1791 – 1811) and the Second Bank of the US (1816 – 1836) each had 20-year charters, and both issued currency, made commercial loans, accepted deposits, purchased securities, had multiple branches, and acted as fiscal agents for the US Treasury.

In both banks the Federal Government was required to purchase 20% of the bank's capital stock and appoint 20% of its directors. Thus majority control was in the hands of private investors who purchased the rest of the stock. The banks were opposed by state-chartered banks, who saw them as very large competitors, and by many who understood them to be banking cartels which compelled to them servitude of the common man.

President Andrew Jackson vetoed legislation to renew the Second Bank of the US, thus starting a period of free banking.

*Resource: Wikipedia

8

THE FOUR LITTLE PIGS AND PENNY PETE

"That Some should be rich shows that others may become rich, and hence is just encouragement to industry and enterprise."
- **Abraham Lincoln (1809 - 1865)**

Seemingly, pigs have been esteemed symbols in many myths and legends the world over. But when, where, and how did coin banks adopt the image of the pig? The short explanation for this customary shape might humor you.

During the Middle Ages, metal was both expensive and hard to find throughout Europe. Consequently, families used clay to create their household pots and jars. Usually the type of clay chosen to make these house wares was a clay called "pygg". Pygg is an orange clay, and it was used widely at this time in Europe because it was inexpensive. Whenever a typical household had coins to save, the elected bank would more than likely be a pygg jar. Inevitably, these pygg jars became known as pygg banks over time.

Later, in the eighteenth century, craftsmen were frequently asked to create pygg banks. Misunderstanding the request, the potters crafted banks in the shape of pigs and painted them likewise. These pig banks soon became popular, and even today *piggy banks* (shaped as pigs) are found around the world throughout diverse cultures.

To get started on your way to increasing your wealth, you need to invite the Four Little Pigs in to your plan. Gather up four piggy banks and mark each one with the following:

Here is a little story about **The Four Little Pigs**...

"Once upon a time four little pigs lived in a village far away. The first little piggy gave all of his money to charity and he never had enough to eat or money for his future. The second little piggy kept all of his money for himself and he had very few friends. The third little piggy put all of his money in investments and oftentimes lost a lot of his money. And the fourth little pig spent all that he earned on snacks, movies and the like.

"These pigs were a terrible sight and could never get ahead. They always struggled with never having enough money to do any of the things they wanted or needed.

"The first little pig invited the second little pig to stay with him so they could give to charity and save for the future by keeping some money. But that didn't seem to solve any of the problems. The first piggy just wanted to give it all away and the second didn't want to spend any of it.

"So the first and second little pigs invited the third pig to join them. Surely this would help solve their problems.

"The third little piggy joined them as he was certain this would help him with his money problems and all the pigs felt glad. But after time, they still could not find peace as the first wanted to give it all away, the second wanted to keep it all and the third wanted to put the money in investments!

"After much discussion and they invited the fourth pig along to join them and still they could not find peace. The first piggy still wanted to

give all the money away to charity, the second piggy wouldn't tell anyone where he was keeping his money, the third piggy was putting his money in to investments while the fourth piggy wanted to spend his on fun things like video games and comic books!

"One day Penny Pete came in to the neighborhood and saw the four little pigs having quite a disagreement in the yard. When Penny Pete saw the sight he just couldn't help but ask what the problem was. He may have wished he had kept on walking. Why, they squealed up such a racket it was hard for Penny Pete to make much sense of it all. However, after he calmed them down and heard their story, he learned quickly that individually they would always struggle, but if they worked together as a team, they might each be able to have what they want and more.

"Penny Pete told them that each of them must play a vital role and do their part if they each want to be happy. The first piggy shall have 10% of all they earned to donate to their church or give to their charity. The second piggy was to take 10% of all they earned or were given and put that in to savings for their future, while the third piggy was to look for and save up for good investments to make their money grow and for this he would have 10% as well from all they earned or was given.

"Finally Penny Pete told the fourth piggy that the rest of the money they earned or were given was for them to share and enjoy. The remaining 70% was for their home, their fun and for all of their needs.

"To the pigs this sounded like a marvelous idea and they quickly began to sort their money and work together as a team. After awhile of some hard work and effort, it became easier for them all to work together and all was well."

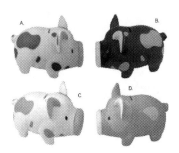

A. **TITHING-CHARITY PIGGY BANK**

B. **PAY YOURSELF-SAVINGS PIGGY BANK**

C. **INVESTMENTS PIGGY BANK**

D. **LIVING EXPENSES PIGGY BANK**

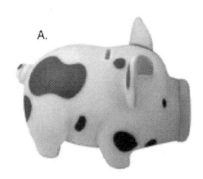

A.

TITHING-CHARITY PIGGY BANK

It is vital that we remember that all money we receive whether as a gift or earned; is a gift from God and we should show gratitude for such a gift. Tithing is a very important investment plan as it teaches us to understand and to realize that having money to buy all of the things we like is a blessing and something that should not go unnoticed.

Giving back is a fundamental lesson plan. None of us will ever get ahead on our own; only through the support of others can we truly get ahead. In doing so, it is important to give back to those who need a hand up. Life has a funny way of throwing curveballs at us from time to time, the very people you see going up the ladder, may very well be the same people you see going down the ladder.

In the TITHING-CHARITY Piggy Bank you must put 10% of all your money earned or given. At the end of each month take it out and make a tithe to your church or find a charity you would like to support and go to them and donate these funds to them each month. This will give you a sense of self-worth and understanding that despite how tough life may seem, you are better than a lot of other people in this world.

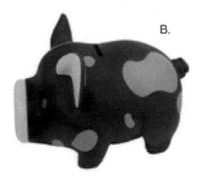

B.

PAY YOURSELF-SAVINGS PIGGY BANK

In Chapter 7 the First Law of Money stated that money will come in increasing quantity to the person who puts no less than 10% of their earnings to create a savings for their future. To start preparing you and helping you develop this critical habit of putting 10% away, the PAY YOURSELF-SAVINGS PIGGY BANK will serve as a reminder to Pay Yourself First!

Watch your parents the next time they sit down to pay their bills after getting their paycheck. See who they pay first and then ask them why? If your parent pays the landlord or mortgage first, ask how much rent or the mortgage is. You will begin to see that most of your parents TIME is spent working for everyone but themselves.

Ask you parents if they pay themselves first? If they say no, ask them why not? If you are the one laboring for the money, shouldn't you get paid first? Far too often we are spending our time working for the Landlord, the Credit Card Company, the Cigarette Company or the State Lottery.

Starting today-10% of all you receive will go in this Piggy Bank.

C.

INVESTMENT PIGGY BANK

"How can I invest money? I'm just a kid!" WRONG! There are plenty of ways to invest your money and yes you may need to find a trustworthy and supportive adult to help you out, but you have to start training your eye to look for investments.

Start building up these funds and over time you will have the opportunity to look at a variety of investments. Perhaps you will save enough to provide the lawnmower and gas to a hard working buddy. Or maybe you will decide to try your own little bubble gum machine business and this money will be there to buy the bubble gum machines and product.

Right now you can't think of investment opportunities because you have not trained yourself to look for them and even if you found them, you wouldn't have the money to get involved in them. Start setting yourself up now to look for opportunities; they are everywhere.

Starting now, put 10% of all you earn or receive in the INVESTMENT PIGGY BANK and start opening your eyes to possibilities.

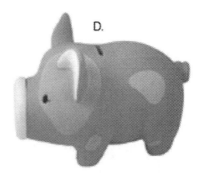

LIVING EXPENSES PIGGY BANK

We all have to live don't we? Let's face it, life without a movie, some soda, or other recreational activities would be a very boring life. Why make money if you can't enjoy it?

The discipline with the LIVING EXPENSES PIGGY BANK is to live within your means. This Piggy Bank will store 70% of all you earn or receive and from this you will live. This will be what you use to buy your new shoes, go to the movies with your friends, get that new video game and pay your bills.

By establishing the discipline to live off of 70% of your earnings you begin to set a proper balance in enjoying today while also building towards a better financial future. Think how far ahead of everyone else you know you will be, if by the time you turned 30 you have $100,000 in the bank, $250,000 in the bank, $500,000 in the bank or even more!

Again, this wouldn't mean you could retire, but it gives you better options in life. Start now, so that later on you can enjoy the finer things life will offer you.

So let's recap the Piggy Banks:

TITHING/CHARITY PIGGY BANK   10%

PAY YOURSELF-SAVING PIGGY BANK   10%

INVESTMENT PIGGY BANK   10%

LIVING EXPENSES PIGGY BANK   70%

Saver Sam

Money Fact!

Fiat Standard of Money

Today, like the currency of most nations, the dollar is fiat money, unbacked by any physical asset. A holder of a Federal Reserve note has no right to demand an asset such as gold or silver from the government in exchange for a note. Consequently, proponents of the intrinsic theory of value believe that the dollar has little intrinsic value (i.e., none except for the value of the paper) and is only valuable as a medium of exchange.

In 1963 the words "Payable to the Bearer on Demand" were removed from all newly issued Federal Reserve Notes. Then, in 1968, redemption of pre-1963 Federal Reserve Notes for gold or silver officially ended. The Coinage Act of 1965 removed all silver from quarters and dimes, which were 90% silver prior to the act.

The content of a nickel has not changed since 1946.

*Resource: Wikipedia

9

ARE YOU INVOLVED OR COMMITTED?

**"Always borrow money from a pessimist; he doesn't expect
to be paid back."**
- Author Unknown

THE STORY OF THE HEN AND THE PIG

A hen and a pig were sauntering down the main street of an old town when they passed a restaurant that advertised "Delicious ham and eggs: 75 cents."

"Sounds like a bargain," approved the hen. "The customers really seem happy with their meals," the hen continued. "I am really glad I can be involved in helping to make those people happy, aren't you glad too, pig?" the hen asked.

"It's all very well for you to be so pleased about the dish, hen," observed the pig with some resentment in his voice. "For you it's all in a day's work and you are only involved in the process; however, for me it represents a FULL commitment," the pig shouted.

This is a timeless story that has been told and retold over the years. Truly the hen was only involved in the process of making people happy with her eggs, while the pig had to really commit and sacrifice for the people to enjoy the ham with their breakfast.

This book has provided ways in which you can start now to begin the process of understanding money, how it works and to earn more of it. We are confident that if you follow the tasks, suggestions and start to think of ways to implement these ideas and incorporate them in your own life, you will undoubtedly be way ahead of the pack in terms of your options in life.

There is however one problem. The only thing we can't guarantee is your commitment. By reading the book you became involved in the process; however, now you must decided whether you will just stay involved in the process or become committed to the process.

The only way to be committed is to take the tools in this book and start putting them in to real practice in your life. Your goal and challenge is to apply these concepts in your home and daily routine.

Will you be involved or committed? The decision is yours.

10

YOUR
FINAL
ASSIGNMENT

EACH ONE TEACH ONE!

It's great that we've provided you with these ideas and strategies so that you can help yourself grow as a financially free person. But just knowing the concepts and strategies will not do you any good unless you begin to put them in to practice.

Every day your parents make decisions based upon doing what they think is best to help you and your family. Your parents worry and work trying to pay the bills and make ends meet so that you have food, water and clothing. It's possible you have parents that aren't involved in your life and we have seen many of these types of situations. Later you will read about Logan who came from such a family situation. And if that is the case; let you be the person who breaks the cycle!

Take the strategies you have learned in this book, go home and sit down with your Mom, Dad, Grandma, Grandpa, Stepparent—whomever you live with and look at the family finances. Try to find out why your family might have money problems; don't just look to find a reason to blame, be on the lookout to discover the cause so that you can begin to work to remedy the situation.

Do they complain they don't have enough money to get through the month? Are they buying lottery tickets, cigarettes, alcohol or other foolish items?

We've talked with many struggling families and upon further investigation, found that although they claim to never have enough money to make it through the month; we've noticed that they play the lottery each week, buy packs of cigarettes daily, drink alcohol, have the internet and cable with premium channels!

If a family stopped spending $5 a day for a pack of cigarettes 365 days per year and put that money in savings, they would have:

$5/day x 365 days per year = $_____(a)

If a family stopped playing the lottery (also known as the 'fool's tax') on a daily basis playing the pick 3, pick 4 or the weekly power balls they would save on average:

$20/week x 52 weeks = $_____(b)

If a family opted to do without HBO, Cinemax, Showtime or any of the other premium cable channels for one year they would increase their savings by:

$15/month x 12 months = $_____(c)

If you and your family decided to give up one 20 oz. soda per day for one year you would have saved:

$1.25/day x 365 days = $_____(d)

If your family made a commitment to cut back on all four of those things for one year, your total family savings would be:

(a)$_____+ (b)$_____ + (c)$_____ +(d)_____ = $_____

Ask your family how having that much money in savings would impact your overall quality of life and future? What could you do with this money after the end of the year and it's all saved up? At the very least, wouldn't it be nice to have that problem to deal with?

Perhaps you could pay off a credit card debt. You could pay off a medical bill. You could pay off the loan on your car or make extra payments to pay off your home mortgage.

All of these ideas will help get you on track to becoming financially free. You were not intended or designed to be in captivity. So much of your families' time is focused on working a job to pay someone else. By making these small sacrifices you can begin to enjoy the benefits later.

Zig Ziglar, a famous author and motivational speaker says, "When you work hard you aren't paying the price—you are enjoying the benefits of your hard labor. You pay a price for not working hard. "When you workout and are in good shape, people say they are paying the price to be in good shape. I say they are wrong. You pay the price if you are in poor shape. You reap the benefits of being in good shape."

Now that you have thought about this, go home, sit down with your family and start asking questions about the household finances. Share what you have learned with your family and see if you all can work together as a team to make life more enjoyable in the future for all of you.

THE PENNY PETE PLEDGE

"I Pledge That Every Penny I Earn Will Be Saved Wisely and Spent Frugally"

As your daily assignment, repeat this Pledge for 30 days every morning. Watch the changes begin in your life.

11

INSPIRATIONAL SUCCESS STORIES

CHRISTOPHER "WHITEY" WHITE

Born and raised in one of the most rural parts of Rhode Island, my nearest neighbor or friend lived miles away. It didn't take long to learn the importance of finding creative ways to entertain myself. I started my first job at 13 and discovered quickly that a man who rolls up his sleeves will never lose his shirt.

After working for two years I saved enough money to buy my first car. Let's be realistic, the best I could afford was a busted out Camaro Z-28 that had been in an accident. I worked for almost a year to fix that car and when it was done, someone offered to buy the car from me for a pretty sizable profit. I was psyched! This one transaction led me to my first real business.

At 15, I started reconditioning cars on the weekend. By the time I was 16 it became Whitey's Motor Sales and Body Shop. I can remember it was suddenly important to pay real close attention to math and accounting classes in school. It was kind of strange to be making more money than the Principal at my high school. Owning this business gave me great experience with fabrication, paints, customization and most importantly, the art of making money. After a few years I decided to sell my company because of an opportunity to move in to the licensed jewelry field.

It was 1990, and a friend of the family asked if I could help him save his struggling but once successful company. This company had made it big a few years before with licensed jewelry for the biggest boy band to date, but when the bands time in the spotlight was over, so was the companies. I saw this as a great challenge.

I took the job as Director of new Product Development. In reality it was more like Director of New Company Development. On my first day I was asked to go to New York City to try and save the licensing rights to make the jewelry that saved the company. Honestly, that was the only opportunity the company had. I had convinced the world's largest entertainment and Media Company that we were the only company that could do their license justice. By 1993 I had become the Executive Vice President and I was only 26!

I put my heart and soul in to this company and I told the owners I wanted to be a Partner in the business and he laughed at me. The owner laughed me out of his office.

I decided I would put my energies in to my own operation. I reached out to a few of my many contacts and within a week I had my own licensed product company (Tri Star Merch), with $4 million of sales already booked in brand new product.

We went international; I worked like a mad man and even made coffee nervous when around me. I took a two year quasi sabbatical and that nearly killed the company. I spent all of 2003 trying to build the business back up, looking for talent, cleaning house and getting passionate again.

On June 8th, 2004 all of the work paid off. I created Gamer Graffix. Everything I had hoped for came in double. It seems I wasn't the only one who was blown away, millions of other people thought our skins rocked!

This time I decided to partner with the best in business; influential people with leadership and contacts. We became so hot we even partnered for a while with famous rapper 50 Cent.

That is my story and a bit about Gamer Graffix. If I can do it, so can you! Keep Chillin' like a Villain!

Whitey

LOGAN REYNOLDS

Logan attended a series of workshops in a community called Oakley; which I (John Keuffer) was hosting. Logan was 12 at the time. The course was a program designed for youth who had low self-esteem and was called *Stick Up For Yourself.*

It was evident that Logan didn't want to be there as he made that quite clear on his first night. In fact, he looked right at me and said, "I don't want to be here, I'm just here because my mom forced me!" I explained to Logan that I was not trying to be Daddy and that if he didn't want to be here, I didn't want him here. After a little stand off, he decided to give the program a try.

Logan stayed through the completion of the program and eventually joined my youth program called Teen Response. Logan's background was hectic at best; very little contact with his father and not good contact with his mother. To say he was a handful would be a gross understatement. Over the years we'd argue about everything, from staying in school to hairstyles. The only thing I could always get Logan to do was read any financial books I had laying around, especially Real Estate investing books.

When he turned 18 he started working on houses; that quickly led to buying foreclosed homes. It wasn't all roses, he had some bad deals and some learning lessons from the experience and quite frankly, I told him to give up and get a job. Can you believe it? Glad he was too stubborn to listen to me. There were weeks when I was worried whether he had food or not and felt he should get a job with steady income. But, Logan was hard headed and kept plugging away.

At the age of 21 he found property along our river that was owned by an elderly man who was medically in bad shape and so was the property. He talked him in to selling the land to him and then went out and found someone with the capital and convinced them to make the purchase and go in to a partnership with him.

Right now on that site they have 10 vacant lots ready for construction and one home already built that is serving as a model home with river views and indoor elevators and a top floor party deck on the homes. Each house is listing for $500,000 each.

Logan has prime real estate along the river; just down the street they are developing land for higher end homes and condos. Now he is just waiting for buyers and poised to dramatically increase his lifestyle.

Logan is only 25 as of 2009. Thank goodness he was stubborn and despite my desire to have him play life safe; he kept plugging away at his dream. I couldn't be more proud of him and humbled at the same time.

APPENDIX

SAMMY'S SUGGESTED READING

Classon, George S. **The Richest Man In Babylon**. New York, New York: Penguin Books USA 1926

Winget, Larry. **How To Write A Book One Page At A Time.** Tulsa, Oklahoma: Win! Publications 1996

Ziglar, Zig. **Raising Positive Kids In A Negative World**. Dallas, Texas: Ziglar Training Systems www.ziglar.com 1985

Ziglar, Zig. **Over The Top**. Dallas, Texas: Ziglar Training Systems www.ziglar.com 1991

Ziglar, Zig. **See You At The Top**. Dallas, Texas: Ziglar Training Systems www.ziglar.com 1975

Ziglar, Zig. **Confessions Of A Happy Christian**. Dallas, Texas: Ziglar Training Systems www.ziglar.com 1978

Winget, Larry. **People Are Idiots And I Can Prove It.** Tulsa, Oklahoma: Win! Publications 2008

Kiyosaki, Robert and Lechter, Sharon. **Rich Dad Poor Dad.** New York, New York: Warner Books ED 2000

APPENDIX

GLOSSARY OF BIG WORDS

Auditor: The person responsible for checking the accuracy of your income statement and your balance sheet.

Asset: Something that puts money in your pocket.

Balance Sheet: A brief synopsis of your assets versus liabilities.

Bankruptcy: When you do not have enough income to pay your bills.

Capital: Cash or something of an agreed upon value.

Cashflow: Cash coming as income and cash going out as an expense.

Certificate of Deposit (CD): A time certificate representing a sum of money deposited for a set length of time at a set rate of interest.

Debt: Money owed to someone else.

Down Payment: A percentage of the purchase price an investor pays for an investment.

Income Statement: A form showing your income and expenses over a period of time.

Liabilities: Amounts of money that is owed to others.

Mortgage: When you finance real estate, the property you are financing is used as collateral or security against the amount of money you are financing.

Mutual Fund: A variety of stocks, bonds, or securities, grouped together and managed by a professional.

Passive Income: Income generated from your investments such as interest, dividends, and real estate rentals with minimal work effort.

ROI: Return On Investment is the return on capital, as an annual percentage, from an investment.

Stock: Ownership in a corporation as a shareholder.

LET'S
MEET
THE
AUTHORS

JOHN R. KEUFFER, III C.C.C.W.

John Keuffer began life in Cincinnati, Ohio; the son of John and Jaynee Keuffer. He has worked as a butcher, stock clerk, bagger, janitor, and loads of other jobs in his lifetime. Once he even shoveled manure when 'sentenced' by his parents to the farm of a friend. Quickly learning that farming and him didn't mix.

In College he did odd jobs, delivered pizza, worked at a convenience store and even worked at a Floral/Landscaping company where he still holds the record for the most plants killed in one day. This would be the only job he would ever quit or be fired at the same time (depending on who tells the story).

John spent ten years working as a Police Officer, starting out as the only white officer in an all African-American community with an all African-American police force. He spent a couple of years in an Appalachian community working as a Police Officer and when he quit; over 5,000 residents signed a petition asking him to stay.

He is the Founder/Director of his own non-profit called Teen Response which he started in 1992. He began his community career as a radio show host on WAIF-FM, WIZF-FM and finally on WCIN-AM and lasted on the air for 12 years in Cincinnati.

Today John is known for his ability to create and run special events, establish non-profit identities for Celebrity Athletes from the NFL, NHL, MLB and even working with members of the WWE. John is known for his loyalty and straight talk and not backing down from most anyone and always saying what's on his mind. John is an actively engaged speaker and talks to over 30,000 youth per year, along with many professional organizations throughout the country. John has won over 60 local, state, national and international honors for his work.

RICHARD CAREY

Richard is a former professional football player whose career spanned 7 years with the Cincinnati Bengals and the Atlanta Falcons. He currently is a certified personal trainer with NSCA, NASM, IFA, AFAA and also Parillo Performance. He has trained and is currently training several high level executives as well as professional, college and high school athletes. He has been training since 1993. He specializes in rapid weight loss through circuit/interval training.

Richard has trained out of Bally's, World Gym and the Y.M.C.A. He is very well respected in his field and community. He founded Personal Trainers World (PTW) in October of 2001. It is currently an 8,000 square-foot multi-use facility located in Northern Cincinnati.

Richard's client base is from age 7 to 84 years of age. Richard's community involvement includes sponsorship for AAU Basketball and AAU Track and Field. He also co-teaches financial literacy with Teen Response to Urban Youth. He is a member of the Fellowship of Christian Athletes (FCA) where he does several speaking engagements through out the year.

His philosophy has always been "Your body is your greatest asset so you must become passionate about staying in shape".

KATHY GARRISON

Kathy (Ferguson) Garrison grew up in Milford, Ohio; one of nine siblings. She knew that nothing came easy and you had to work for what you wanted. She was employed by one company all of her working career, Procter & Gamble. She retired in 2002 after 40 years of service. This exemplary community supporter and role model has given many years of dedication and generosity to the betterment of both community and its youth.

Gleaned from her time and experiences with youth, Kathy has committed herself to identifying and supporting effective grassroots efforts that provide not only scholarships but trainings to encourage excellence, self-improvement, and "personal best" to many children. Her "lessons of life" are a source of hope to all who dare to dream their boldest dreams.

Kathy holds board positions with Millcreek Habitat for Humanity, Students Concerned About Today and Tomorrow. She is the previous President of the Madisonville Community Council and past board member of the Madisonville Arts Center. She is the founder and Executive Director of Madisonville Weed & Seed Sustained, Inc. since 2007. Kathy was also the Site Coordinator for the National Award Winning Madisonville Weed & Seed under the Department of Justice from 2003 to 2007 for its partnerships and work with youth. She consults with other locations that would like to become Weed & Seed Sites and she also helps facilitate trainings for women.

Kathy is considered a neighborhood leader who exemplifies the imagination, courage, determination, and self-help ethics necessary to renew communities and reach our youth.

SPECIAL
OFFER
JUST FOR YOU!

Hey friends! For our new fans and readers of this book only; if you go to the Gamer Graffix website: www.gamergraffix.com and scroll to the bottom of the page and click on affiliates; sign up to be an affiliate.

Where it asks:

SAVER SAMMY

Just type in '**Saver Sammy**' for special recognition.

What a great way for a young person to learn on a no-risk scale about starting, marketing and promoting a business!

Special thanks to our friends at Gamer Graffix for their support.

WWW.GAMERGRAFFIX.COM

DISCLAIMER

No part of this book or its contents is intended to provide either legal, accounting or tax advice to the reader of this book.

As with all advice, you should seek professional counsel when it comes to all legal matters, accounting matters and tax matters.

PLEASE SEND YOUR COMMENTS

Teen Response, Inc.
PO Box 9555
Cincinnati, OH 45209-0555
john@teenresponse.org

Name: (Please Print)_____

Address: _____

City/State/Zip: _____

Phone: _____ Email: _____

Grade: _____ Age: _____

Comments:

_____

_____

_____

_____

_____

_____

_____

_____

_____

_____

_____

_____

_____

_____

_____

_____

_____

_____

_____

_____